Reproducible Resource

Bullying

> **Identify**

> **Cope**

> **Prevent**

Grades 5 – 6

World Teachers Press®

www.worldteacherspress.com

Published with the permission of R.I.C. Publications Pty. Ltd.

First published by R.I.C. Publications Pty. Ltd., Perth, Western Australia. Revised by Didax Educational Resources.

Printed in the United States of America.

Order Number 2-5215
ISBN 978-1-58324-157-8

D E F G H 10 09 08 07 06

395 Main Street
Rowley, MA 01969
www.didax.com

Foreword

Bullying has been likened by some commentators to lifestyle physical ailments prevalent in modern society, such as obesity, smoking-related disease, heart disease and even skin cancers. The "likeness" is that, in a majority of cases, adequate and appropriate preventive measures will stop the condition from arising altogether. All too often, bullying is treated as a condition only after it manifests itself, rather than pre-emptively, before it actually arises.

Bullying is a complex issue. It requires an ongoing education of students to develop skills and strategies to allow them to IDENTIFY, COPE with and, ultimately, PREVENT bullying from occurring.

This series provides developmental activities to promote positive attitudes in students, forestalling the development of injurious, bullying behavior.

Titles in this series:
> *Bullying,* Grades 3–4
> *Bullying,* Grades 5–6
> *Bullying,* Grades 7–8

Contents

Teacher's Notes

Each student page is supported by a teacher's page which provides the following information.

Specific **indicators** explain what the students are expected to demonstrate through completing the activities.

Teacher information provides the teacher with detailed additional information to supplement the student page.

Did You Know? is a collection of background information on bullying behavior, covering interesting statistics and informative research facts.

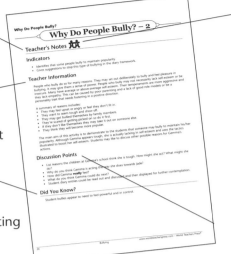

The icons below indicate the focus of each activity. Some activities may have more than one icon.

 Activities to assist students to **identify** bullying behavior and why people bully.

 Activities to help students **cope** with bullying behavior.

 Activities where students learn strategies to **prevent** bullying behavior in themselves and/or others.

Discussion Points have been suggested to further develop ideas on the student page.

Each book is divided into four sections.

What Is Bullying? (pages 14 – 23)

The activities in this section give students opportunities to identify what bullying is and the various forms it can take.

Most definitions of bullying agree:
- It is deliberately hurtful, either physically or psychologically.
- It is repeated often over time.
- It is difficult for the person being bullied to defend himself/herself against it – he/she is weaker physically or psychologically.

Bullying can be divided into three types:
1. Physical – including hitting, punching, shoving, pinching, tripping, spitting, scratching, damaging, hiding or stealing belongings, throwing objects at someone, or locking someone in or out
2. Verbal – name-calling, making offensive remarks, taunting, teasing, put-downs
3. Emotional – spreading rumors, gossiping about or embarrassing someone, making fun of someone, using threatening looks or gestures, excluding or threatening to exclude from groups, ignoring, ostracizing, or alienating

Note: In each level of *Bullying*, the word "bully" is used as a verb and not a noun. In this way, the bullying behavior is emphasized and not the child. Instead of labeling a child a "bully," he/she is referred to as "a person who bullies."

Why Do People Bully? (pages 24 – 35)

People bully for a wide variety of reasons. These include feeling they don't fit in, disliking themselves, peer pressure, wanting to show off, feeling upset or angry, or having a fear of being bullied themselves. This is not necessarily due to low self-esteem or insecurity; in fact, it can be quite the opposite. However, most people who bully have a lack of empathy, which can be caused by poor parenting, a lack of good role models, or be a personality trait that needs fostering in a positive direction.

In this section, students are encouraged to explore and discuss bullying scenarios and consider possible reasons for each. Teachers will also find useful activities to help them work on anger management with students. In addition, students will learn that those who bully vary widely in physical appearance and background.

Teacher's Notes

How Does Bullying Make You Feel? (pages 36 – 45)

The activities in this section emphasize the importance of respecting the feelings and emotions of others. They require students to "put themselves in the shoes" of the person being bullied and the person who is bullying. Students are encouraged to empathize with others and to understand and deal with their own feelings. The peer group which supports and reinforces the bullying behavior is also encouraged to develop empathy for the person being bullied.

The advantages of using this approach include:
- Everyone gains a clear understanding of what bullying is.
- The focus is on finding a solution and not finding someone to blame.
- The person being bullied is able to express his or her feelings and deal with the situation.
- When people around develop empathy for the person being bullied, the dynamics of the situation change.
- Many instances of bullying rely on keeping information quiet. However, where the feelings on bullying are known to everybody it is harder for the bullying practices to continue.
- Understanding the feelings of all involved can help lay the foundations for proactive prevention of potential bullying situations.

It is recommended that a set of rules on speaking and listening be established in the classroom, with students given the chance to regularly discuss a variety of subjects so an environment exists where they feel safe to express their feelings. If such a safe environment exists, the discussion sections accompanying each activity should produce better results and maximum participation.

What Can You Do? (pages 46 – 65)

This section of the book provides different strategies to help students cope with and prevent bullying behavior. It offers activities that promote a school ethos where bullying is openly discussed and seen as unacceptable behavior. Students are given the opportunity to discuss tolerance and friendship and to learn strategies to promote communication, problem solving and conflict resolution. Those students who are assertive and can discuss their feelings will develop a higher self-esteem and are less likely to become victims or people who bully.

Teaching problem-solving strategies through discussion and role-playing will assist students to learn and develop skills for positive social behaviors and relationships. Beginning sentences with "I" statements, having confident body language and being assertive without becoming aggressive, can be very effective ways of letting someone who is showing bullying behavior know that his/her actions will not be tolerated. Teachers can help by running drama sessions where students participate in exercises where they need to stand confidently, use eye contact and speak clearly. Deep breathing to relax the body can also help.

Students can be taught to use other strategies to deal with bullying behavior, such as avoiding the situation whenever possible and knowing when to ask for help. Asking for help is essential, especially for victims who are not able to attempt the strategies above or for those who have tried these techniques and find they are not working. Some bullying situations can be stopped early on before the bullying cycle begins through intervention by peers, teachers, parents, or other adults.

Teacher's Notes

Working with Parents

Support from parents is vitally important to help encourage a "non-bullying" environment in the classroom or school. Parental approval is very important to students and most parents are eager to support anti-bullying programs. Parents are also often the first to detect signs that their child is being bullied or is bullying others.

Teachers can encourage parents to become involved by:
- encouraging open communication
- providing bullying information and statistics
- encouraging them to watch for signs that their child is involved in a bullying situation, and to report it as soon as possible
- taking parents' concerns about bullying seriously
- asking them to discourage their child from using bullying behavior
- giving advice on how to solve conflict without violence or aggression
- encouraging them to talk to their child about what is happening at school

Tips for Creating a Non-bullying School Environment

Much has been documented and written on the subject of bullying and findings between schools may differ. However, the approach universally agreed on is that for schools to successfully and effectively tackle the problem of bullying, a whole-school approach is needed.

Successful anti-bullying initiatives have included the following:
- Include teachers, students, administration staff, parents and even the wider community in the consultation process, and the development and implementation of policy.
- Collect information about bullying in your school and define a whole-school philosophy.
- Create a written policy document that presents a mission statement, the rights and responsibilities of students, teachers and parents, and the procedures.
- Make the policy well known.
- Ensure active supervision on the school grounds and help create situations that teach students how to play and interact together.
- Acknowledge the important role that bystanders can play in reducing bullying.
- Teach non-aggressive strategies such as problem-solving and conflict-resolution skills.
- Continually monitor and maintain the policy.
- Create team-based social relationships at the class level and encourage participation by all students. Provide opportunities for all students to get to know each other well.
- Measure social relationships between students at a class-level and be aware of potential bullying problems.
- Be aware of early warning signs.

Teacher's Notes

Explanations of the generic pages included in this book are outlined below:

The *Incident Report* (page 8) can be used by teachers and support staff to record bullying incidents. The teacher can detail any procedures that are introduced as a result of the event and keep records of parental involvement and follow-up actions.

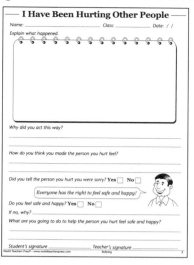

I Have Been Hurting Other People (page 9) is designed to be completed by students who have instigated or participated in bullying behavior. The student describes the incident in pictures or words and explains his or her actions. The student is asked to consider the feelings of the person(s) they have hurt. It also allows the student to assess how he or she is feeling.

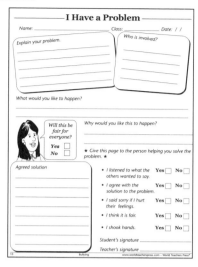

I Have a Problem (page 10) is constructed for students who have experienced bullying behavior. The student explains the problem and describes how he or she would like it to be solved. The second half of the page requires both parties involved in the problem to agree on a solution.

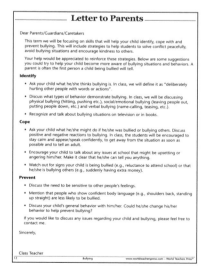

This *Questionnaire* (page 11) can be used by teachers to reveal individual or class perceptions about bullying and its existence in the school. It also provides the students with an opportunity to consider who is responsible for stopping bullying in their school.

A *Letter to Parents* (page 12) is provided to inform and gain the support of parents and caregivers concerning bullying behavior.

Merit Certificates (page 13) are included to recognize and promote positive behavior.

Incident Report

Student name: _____ Date: / /

Class: _____ Teacher: _____

Teacher/Support Staff reporting the incident: _____

Where did the incident occur? _____

Behavior displayed: Bullying ☐ Being bullied ☐

physical bullying	verbal bullying	emotional/social bullying
☐ hitting, punching	☐ teasing/name calling	☐ leaving people out
☐ pinching, tripping	☐ making offensive remarks	☐ spreading rumors
☐ kicking, pushing	☐ making discriminatory remarks	☐ excluding someone
☐ scratching, spitting	☐ insulting someone	☐ ignoring someone
☐ damaging/stealing property	☐ threatening someone	☐ making fun of someone
☐ throwing objects at someone	☐ repeated teasing	☐ stopping people from befriending someone
☐ hiding/taking belongings	☐ intimidating someone	
☐ other	☐ other	☐ other
_____	_____	_____

Comments:

_____

_____

_____

Actions taken after the incident:

Parents informed: yes ☐ no ☐ Date: / /

_____

_____

Follow up: Date: / /

_____

_____

Parent's signature _____ *Teacher's signature* _____

I Have Been Hurting Other People

Name: _____ Class: _____ Date: / /

Explain what happened.

Why did you act this way?

_____

_____

How do you think you made the person you hurt feel?

_____

_____

Did you tell the person you hurt you were sorry? **Yes** ☐ **No** ☐

Everyone has the right to feel safe and happy!

Do you feel safe and happy? **Yes** ☐ **No** ☐

If no, why? _____

What are you going to do to help the person you hurt feel safe and happy?

_____

_____

Student's signature _____ Teacher's signature _____

I Have a Problem

Name: _____ Class: _____ Date: / /

Explain your problem.

_____

_____

_____

_____

_____

Who is involved?

_____

_____

_____

_____

What would you like to happen?

_____

_____

Will this be fair for everyone?

Yes ☐

No ☐

Why would you like this to happen?

_____

_____

★ Give this page to the person helping you solve the problem. ★

Agreed solution:

_____

_____

_____

_____

_____

_____

_____

- I listened to what the others wanted to say.   **Yes** ☐   **No** ☐

- I agree with the solution to the problem.   **Yes** ☐   **No** ☐

- I said sorry if I hurt their feelings.   **Yes** ☐   **No** ☐

- I think it is fair.   **Yes** ☐   **No** ☐

- I shook hands.   **Yes** ☐   **No** ☐

Student's signature _____

Teacher's signature _____

Questionnaire

School: _____ Date: / /

Boy ☐ Girl ☐ Age:_____

❶ Have you ever been bullied at this school?

☐ never ☐ a few times ☐ about once a week ☐ more than once a week

❷ What type of bullying?

☐ been teased ☐ been left out ☐ been hit, kicked, pinched, punched, or shoved

☐ been called names ☐ had my things damaged or stolen ☐ been sworn at

☐ received a mean letter ☐ other, such as _____

❸ Where did the bullying take place?

☐ in the classroom ☐ on the playground ☐ in the bathroom

☐ outside the school ☐ other

❹ Who did you tell?

☐ teacher ☐ friend ☐ parent ☐ no one ☐ other

❺ Have you ever seen bullying at this school?

☐ never ☐ a few times ☐ about once a week ☐ more than once a week

❻ What type of bullying have you seen?

☐ teasing ☐ leaving out ☐ hitting, kicking, pinching, punching, or shoving

☐ name-calling ☐ damaging or stealing things ☐ swearing

☐ receiving a mean letter ☐ other, such as _____

❼ Where did the bullying take place?

☐ in the classroom ☐ on the playground ☐ in the bathroom

☐ outside the school ☐ other

❽ Who did you tell?

☐ teacher ☐ friend ☐ parent ☐ no one ☐ other

❾ Who do you think should be responsible for stopping bullying?

☐ person bullying ☐ teachers ☐ principal

☐ parents of person bullying ☐ parents of victim

Letter to Parents

Dear Parents/Guardians/Caretakers,

This term we will be focusing on skills that will help your child identify, cope with and prevent bullying. This will include strategies to help students to solve conflict peacefully, avoid bullying situations and encourage kindness to others.

Your help would be appreciated to reinforce these strategies. Below are some suggestions you could try to help your child become more aware of bullying situations and behaviors. A parent is often the first person a child being bullied will tell.

Identify

- Ask your child what he/she thinks bullying is. In class, we will define it as "deliberately hurting other people with words or actions."

- Discuss what types of behavior demonstrate bullying. In class, we will be discussing physical bullying (hitting, pushing etc.), social/emotional bullying (leaving people out, putting people down, etc.) and verbal bullying (name-calling, teasing, etc.).

- Recognize and talk about bullying situations on television or in books.

Cope

- Ask your child what he/she might do if he/she was bullied or bullying others. Discuss positive and negative reactions to bullying. In class, the students will be encouraged to stay calm and act and speak confidently, to get away from the situation as soon as possible and to tell an adult.

- Encourage your child to talk about any issues at school that might be upsetting or angering him/her. Make it clear that he/she can tell you anything.

- Watch out for signs your child is being bullied (e.g., reluctance to attend school) or that he/she is bullying others (e.g., suddenly having extra money).

Prevent

- Discuss the need to be sensitive to other people's feelings.

- Mention that people who show confident body language (e.g., shoulders back, standing up straight) are less likely to be bullied.

- Discuss your child's general behavior with him/her. Could he/she change his/her behavior to help prevent bullying?

If you would like to discuss any issues regarding your child and bullying, please feel free to contact me.

Sincerely,

Class Teacher

What A Great Group!

For: _____

Group Name: _____

Date: _____ Signed: _____

Friendship Award

For:

_____

_____

Name: _____

Date: _____ Signed: _____

WOW

Great Achievement

in

_____

_____

Name: _____

Date: _____ Signed: _____

What Is Bullying? – 1

Teacher's Notes 👤

Indicators

- Understands what the term "bullying" means.
- Identifies examples of physical, social and verbal bullying in a variety of situations.

Teacher Information

Most definitions of bullying agree:
- It is deliberately hurtful (physically or psychologically).
- It is repeated often over time.
- It is difficult for the person being bullied to defend himself/herself against it – he/she is weaker physically or psychologically.

Bullying can be divided into three types:
1. Physical – hitting, punching, pinching, tripping, spitting, kicking, pushing, scratching, damaging, hiding or taking belongings
2. Verbal – name-calling, making offensive remarks, insulting someone.
3. Social – spreading rumors/nasty stories about someone, making fun of someone, excluding from groups, ignoring, ostracizing, alienating

Discussion Points

- Brainstorm words to describe bullying with the class to assist students with Questions 1 and 3 on page 17.
- Ask students for further examples of bullying under the headings "physical," "social" and "verbal." (Refer to teacher information.)
- Read each scenario to the class or ask individual students to read. Allow students to read each again by themselves.
- To assist students with Question 2 on page 17, ask for keywords and phrases to write a summary on the board of what each child in the scenarios did when he/she was bullied.
- Ask students what they think the worst type of bullying was in the four scenarios and why.

Did You Know?

The most common form of bullying is verbal.

What Is Bullying? – 1

Bullying is deliberately hurting other people with words or actions. Bullying can be physical, verbal, or social.

Physical bullying can mean hitting, kicking, pushing, or tripping someone.

Social bullying can mean leaving people out, making people feel frightened, or putting people down.

Verbal bullying can mean name-calling or teasing.

Read each of these stories. Highlight who is doing the bullying in each story.

Story A

Anna arrives at a new school. She doesn't know anybody. Her teacher asks two girls in her class to play with her at recess. But when Anna tries to talk to them, they pretend they can't hear her. Anna spends the rest of recess hiding in the bathroom.

Story B

The first day Tom comes to school wearing glasses, he and his friend Jamie go outside at lunchtime to play basketball. Two other boys call him "four-eyes" and knock his glasses from his face. Jamie doesn't say anything and goes off to get a drink. Tom tries to ignore the boys, but ends up yelling at them, which only makes them laugh.

Story C

Every Monday Kristy comes to school, she is met by a group of older boys who push her and take her lunch money. The only time the boys don't do this is when Kristy manages to walk in the school gate with a group of friends. She is too afraid of the boys to tell an adult.

Story D

Hardly anyone in David's class wants to sit next to him. He is not sure why, but a lot of children whisper to each other while looking at him and then laugh. They always manage to do this while the teacher isn't looking. David decides to spread a nasty rumor about Emily, the person he thinks started this behavior, and soon many of his classmates don't want to sit next to her, either.

What Is Bullying? – 2

Teacher's Notes

Indicators

- Brainstorms words to describe bullying and bullying behavior.
- Suggests alternative behavior for victims of different bullying situations.

Teacher Information

Most definitions of bullying agree:
- It is deliberately hurtful (physically or psychologically).
- It is repeated often over time.
- It is difficult for the person being bullied to defend himself/herself against it – he/she is weaker physically or psychologically.

Bullying can be divided into three types:
1. Physical – hitting, punching, pinching, tripping, spitting, kicking, pushing, scratching, damaging, hiding or taking belongings.
2. Verbal – name-calling, making offensive remarks, insulting someone.
3. Social – spreading rumors/nasty stories about someone, making fun of someone, excluding from groups, ignoring, ostracizing, alienating.

Discussion Points

- If some groups are having difficulty with suggestions of alternative behavior for each victim, some examples to give them could be:
  Anna – Instead of hiding in the bathroom she could have ignored the girls and gone looking for another pair or small group of girls she recognized from the class.
  Tom – Instead of yelling he could have firmly told them not to do that and continued playing basketball.
  David – He could have asked Emily why she was behaving this way.
  Kristy – She could have told an adult she could trust to help solve this problem.
- Discuss the variety of alternatives each group offers and the "pros" and "cons" for each.
- Students could role-play each scenario and alternative.

Did You Know?

The most common form of verbal bullying is name-calling.

What Is Bullying? – 2

Find a group of three to four people. You will need to refer to page 15 to answer and discuss these questions. When you have finished, report back to the class.

❶ Brainstorm 10 words that your group feels best describe bullying.

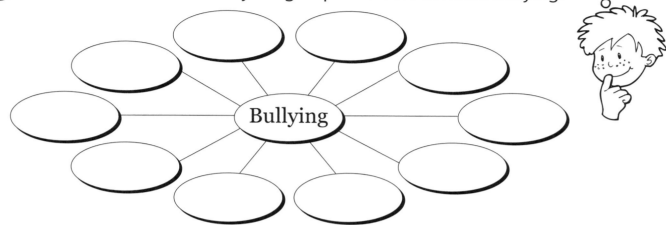

Bullying

❷ Discuss what each child on page 15 did when he/she was bullied. Write what else each could have done.

Anna

Tom

Kristy

David

❸ Write words to describe the behavior of the friends or classmates in the last three stories.

(Story b) _____

(Story c) _____

(Story d) _____

❹ Make up a short bullying story in your groups. Read it to the class and discuss what type of bullying it is.

Bullying on the Playground

Teacher's Notes

Indicators

- Portrays different characters in a play about bullying to experience how the victim and the person bullying would feel.
- Decides on the best ending to the play through acting out and discussion.

Teacher Information

In elementary schools, most bullying takes place on the playground. Name-calling, exclusion from groups and telling "secrets" while the victim is watching are common forms of bullying, as demonstrated in the play.

When students act out the play and the alternative endings, allow them to experience being both the victim and one of the students bullying.

Discussion Points

- How does each character in the play feel? What expression would he/she have on his/her face? How would he/she be sitting or standing? (Slouched? head down or up? hands on hips?, etc.) List suggestions on the board to prepare them for acting out the plays.
- After reading the two endings, allow students to discuss each situation in their group and make suggestions as to what child A should do next. Discuss all suggestions – how many are similar?

Did You Know?

Most bullying takes place in or close to school buildings.

Bullying on the Playground

1 Read and act out this play with a group of three. Try both endings. Use facial expressions and movements to show how the characters are feeling.

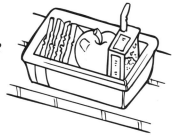

Scene: A school playground at lunchtime.
A, carrying a lunch box, walks up to B and C, who are sitting on a bench, eating their lunch. When they see A they both stop. B whispers something to C, who laughs.

A Hi. Can I sit with you today?
B *(sticking leg out)* There's no room.
C Yeah, and besides, we don't sit with people who ... *(Whispers the last part of the sentence to B. B and C laugh.)*
A Who what? I haven't done anything.
B Why don't you go sit with someone else ... if you can find anyone!
C *(pointing at A)* Oh, look, I think the baby is going to cry!

Now try adding these two endings.

A I'm not going to cry. I can find plenty of people who want to play with me.
B Not if we've told them all about you.
C Yeah, everyone knows about it.
A I'm not listening to you any more. If you want to make things up about me, go ahead. My real friends wouldn't believe it anyway.
(A walks away from B and C.)

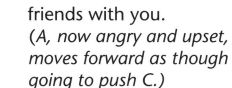
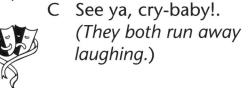

A That's not fair. I just want to be your friend.
B Well, no, thanks.
C We don't want to be friends with you.
(A, now angry and upset, moves forward as though going to push C.)
B Temper, temper!
C See ya, cry-baby!.
(They both run away laughing.)

2 In your groups, discuss which was the better way for A to have dealt with the situation, and what A could do next if the bullying continues.

3 Think about a bullying situation you have been involved in or have seen. Write a short bullying play in your groups on a separate sheet of paper. Try adding a different ending!

Who Gets Bullied?

Teacher's Notes

Indicators

- Understands some reasons why someone may be bullied and whether those reasons are acceptable.
- Realizes no one is exactly the same and everyone has a right to be valued.

Teacher Information

Everyone has the right to be valued for their individuality, including race, sex, culture, and physical and intellectual differences.

Tolerance of others is the key focus of this lesson.

Group work, such as the activity on page 21, is a way to promote cooperative learning and tolerance and help break the bully/victim cycle. Each member of the group adds to the activity, his/her contribution is valued and the group's results are shared with peers.

Discussion Points

- Are there any good reasons for bullying someone?
- Is it all right to bully someone because he/she looks different or likes to do different things?
- Collate students' suggestions for Question 1(a) and discuss.
- Students should report back to the class in their group and share the answers to Question 3.

Did You Know?

One in seven children is either someone who bullies or a victim of bullying.

Who Gets Bullied?

Bullying can happen to anyone. People can be bullied because of their likes or dislikes, the way they look, or what they believe—or sometimes for no reason at all.

But no one deserves to be bullied or to feel ashamed of who they are. The problem is with the person doing the bullying, not with the person being bullied.

1 (a) Write some reasons why people might be bullied; e.g. being tall or short, wearing unusual clothing, etc.

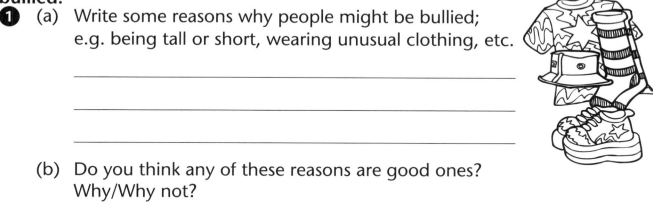

_____

_____

_____

    (b) Do you think any of these reasons are good ones? Why/Why not?

_____

_____

2 Find out how people in your class are different and similar. Make a group of three people. The other two people in your group should be people you don't know very well. Discuss your likes and dislikes, the way you look (e.g. hair color) and any other details (e.g., place of birth).

    (a) List five things you all have in common.

    (b) List three things about you that were different from the other two people in your group.

    (c) Write something you found out about a person in your group that you admire or like.

Where Does Bullying Happen?

Teacher's Notes 👤

Indicators

- Realizes how and why someone who bullies attempts to keep bullying a secret from adults.
- Understands the terms "leader," "follower" and "peer pressure."

Teacher Information

Students who witness bullying may act in the following ways:
- Help the person bullying by joining in.
- Help the person bullying by watching, laughing, or shouting encouragement.
- Remain completely uninvolved.
- Help the person being bullied by telling the person bullying to stop or getting an adult, etc.

Bullying usually happens where the person doing the bullying has an "audience" of other children. It might be people they don't know or a group of their friends. If adults are nearby, though, bullies can be very careful to not let them see what they are doing.

When a group of people bully, there is often a "leader" and "followers" who go along with what the leader is doing or saying. Sometimes the followers do not really agree with what the leader is doing, but might feel that they have to. This is sometimes called "peer pressure."

Openly discussing ways for students to assist others who are being bullied will help foster an anti-bullying attitude in the school.

Keeping bullying a secret from adults gives the person bullying more power to continue. That is why they go to so much trouble to keep it from the view of adults and attempt to stop the victims from telling.

Discussion Points

- Ask the students for keywords and phrases to help define the meaning of "leader," "follower" and the term "peer pressure."
- Ask students to think about if they have been a leader and/or a follower and if they have experienced peer pressure. (Students should not have to explain to the class – just contemplate to assist in answering questions.)
- Questions 1, 2 and 3 could be discussed as a whole class after answering individually. The cartoon strips could be displayed at the teacher's discretion only if students wish. Otherwise, the teacher could collect them and talk about a selection, while maintaining anonymity.

Extra Discussion Points
- How does it feel to watch someone being bullied?
- Does that make that person as bad as the person bullying?
- What do you think stops people from helping the person being bullied?

Did You Know?

About 75-80% of students in surveys said they would not join in or would like to help the bullied child.

Where Does Bullying Happen?

Bullying usually happens where the person doing the bullying has an "audience" of other children. It might be people they don't know or a group of their friends. If adults are nearby, though, bullies can be very careful at not letting them see what they are doing.

When a group of people bully, there is often a "leader" and "followers" who go along with what the leader is doing or saying. Sometimes, the followers do not really agree with what the leader is doing, but feel that they have to. This is usually called "peer pressure."

❶ Name three places at your school where bullying might take place.

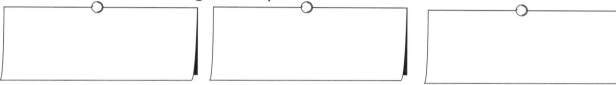

❷ What might be some ways a bully could avoid being seen by an adult?

_____

_____

❸ What might be some reasons a "follower" might feel he/she has to support a bully?

_____

_____

❹ Draw a cartoon strip of four pictures showing an example of peer pressure.

Why Do People Bully? – 1

Teacher's Notes 🏃

Indicators

- Identifies some reasons people may bully.
- Recognizes that people who bully may be hiding how they really feel.

Teacher Information

People who bully do so for many reasons. They may set out deliberately to bully and feel pleasure in bullying. It may give them a sense of power. People who bully may not necessarily lack self-esteem or be insecure. Many have average or above-average self-esteem. Their temperaments are more aggressive and they lack empathy. This can be caused by poor parenting and a lack of good role models or be a personality trait that needs fostering in a positive direction.

A summary of reasons includes:
- They may feel upset or angry or feel they don't fit in.
- They want to seem tough and show off.
- They may get bullied themselves by family members.
- They're scared of getting picked on so they do it first.
- If they don't like themselves they may take it out on someone else.
- They think they will become more popular.

Children (or adults) who bully others can come from any kind of family, regardless of social class or cultural background.

People who bully vary in their physical appearance as do the people they bully. A person's actions identify him/her as one who bullies.

Discussion Points

- Draw a picture of a person's head and hair – but not the face. Ask the students to imagine that this is someone who bullies. Ask them to describe what he/she looks like, what he/she likes to do, friends, behavior, etc. (In this way, no student will be singled out as an example, either correctly or incorrectly, as someone who bullies.)
- Discuss:
    Why did you choose those characteristics?
    Why do you think this person bullies?
    Do you think that this person may have been bullied? Why/Why not?
    Do you think that this person realizes he/she bullies?
    Do you think this person's friends really like him/her?
    Do you think this person likes bullying? Sometimes? Always?
    Do you think this person is happy? Unhappy? Why?
- The student answers to the worksheet could be discussed when complete.

Did You Know?

Children involved in bullying (whether bullying or being bullied) usually have poor social skills and problems at home.

Why Do People Bully? – 1

Do people bully simply because they are mean? No! There are many reasons why people bully. These might have to do with their feelings, or how other people, especially their friends and family, treat them. Sometimes, people might not even realize they are bullying someone!

1 Brainstorm reasons why people might bully others.

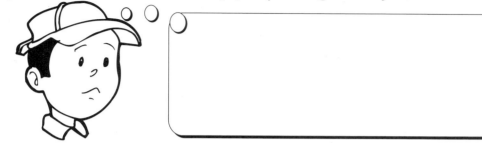

2 How do you think someone could bully someone else without realizing it?

3 People who are being bullied often think that it would great to be a bully! But people who bully are often not all they seem. Match the sentences below.

People who bully might be surrounded by people but these people ...	what they say is hurtful until they are told.
People who bully may hurt you with what they say but they may not realize ...	hurting others does not make you feel good inside.
It might look like the person who is bullying feels good about it but ...	often they are just pretending.
People who bully might look happy but often they are hiding ...	how unhappy they feel.
People who bully might seem tough but ...	might not be real friends.

Why Do People Bully? – 2

Teacher's Notes

Indicators

- Identifies that some people bully to maintain popularity.
- Gives suggestions to stop this type of bullying in the diary framework.

Teacher Information

People who bully do so for many reasons. They may set out deliberately to bully and feel pleasure in bullying. It may give them a sense of power. People who bully may not necessarily lack self-esteem or be insecure. Many have average or above-average self-esteem. Their temperaments are more aggressive and they lack empathy. This can be caused by poor parenting and a lack of good role models or be a personality trait that needs fostering in a positive direction.

A summary of reasons includes:
- They may feel upset or angry or feel they don't fit in.
- They want to seem tough and show off.
- They may get bullied themselves by family members.
- They're scared of getting picked on so do it first.
- If they don't like themselves they may take it out on someone else.
- They think they will become more popular.

The main aim of this activity is to demonstrate to the students that someone may bully to maintain his/her popularity. Although Gemma appears tough, she is actually lacking in self-esteem and uses the tactics illustrated to boost her self-esteem. Students may like to discuss other possible reasons for Gemma's actions.

Discussion Points

- List reasons the children at Gemma's school think she is tough. How might she act? What might she do?
- Why do you think Gemma is acting the way she does towards Jade?
- How did Gemma **really** feel?
- What do you think Gemma could do next?
- Student diary entries could be read out and discussed and then displayed for further contemplation.

Did You Know?

Student bullies appear to need to feel powerful and in control.

Why Do People Bully? – 2

The children at Gemma's school think she is tough—she certainly acts that way. She often picks on people who are new.

Dear Diary

People think I'm tough, but only you know the truth.

The new girl, Jade, arrived three days ago and she's far from being the frightened new kid. She's pretty, and already knows some people in the class.

I was frightened that people might like her better than me, so I *decided to do something about it.*

During recess, I said nasty things about her hair and clothes and some other kids nearby laughed at her with me. She looked like she was going to cry.

The strange thing is, I don't feel good about doing this, but I feel like I can't stop now.

What should I do?

Gemma

Imagine Gemma's diary has a magical ability to write back to her! What advice do you think it would give her? Write a reply as the diary.

Dear Gemma

_____

_____

_____

_____

_____

_____

_____

_____

_____

Your Diary

Why Do People Bully? – 3

Teacher's Notes

Indicators

- Identifies that some people bully due to peer pressure.
- Gives suggestions to stop this type of bullying.

Teacher Information

People who bully do so for many reasons. They may set out deliberately to bully and feel pleasure in bullying. It may give them a sense of power. People who bully may not necessarily lack self-esteem or be insecure. Many have average or above-average self-esteem. Their temperaments are more aggressive and they lack empathy. This can be caused by poor parenting and a lack of good role models or be a personality trait that needs fostering in a positive direction.

A summary of reasons includes:
- They may feel upset or angry or feel they don't fit in.
- They want to seem tough and show off.
- They may get bullied themselves by family members.
- They're scared of getting picked on so do it first.
- If they don't like themselves they may take it out on someone else.
- They think they will become more popular.

The main aim of this activity is to demonstrate to the students that someone may bully due to peer pressure. John wants to become part of the popular group at school. He wants to show this group he is not a part of the group with Craig, Sam and Daniel. He uses the tactics as they are told by the boys to prove this. Students may like to discuss the possible reasons for John's actions.

Discussion Points

- Why do you think John is behaving this way?
- Is John bullying? Explain.
- Do you think Craig, Sam, or Daniel have done anything wrong?
- Do you think the problem can be solved?
- How has the teacher helped so far? Can the teacher do anything else to help?
- Students could role-play this situation with the best case and worst case scenarios written in Question 2.

Did You Know?

Students who bully become less popular as they grow older, until they are eventually disliked by the majority of students.

Why Do People Bully? – 3

Craig and his two friends, Sam and Daniel, have a problem with their friend, John. Sometimes he acts like he is their friend, but at other times he does things which make them feel unhappy. Their teacher asks each of boys separately to explain what is happening.

> **Craig:** I think John is only pretending to be my friend. He often talks about me behind my back to other kids.

> **Sam:** I think John is embarrassed to be friends with us. When other kids walk by, he sometimes pushes me and says horrible things about me.

> **Daniel:** John has started to wear the same types of clothes as the more popular kids. Sometimes he's nice to me, but only when we're on our own. I'm sick of it.

1 Write what you think John would say about what is happening.

2 Think about what might end up happening in this situation.

(a) What would be the worst thing that could happen?

(b) What would be the best thing that could happen?

(c) What do you think will actually happen?

Why Do People Bully? – 4

Teacher's Notes

Indicators

- Identifies that some people bully because they are jealous of others.
- Gives suggestions to stop this type of bullying.

Teacher Information

People who bully do so for many reasons. They may set out deliberately to bully and feel pleasure in bullying. It may give them a sense of power. People who bully may not necessarily lack self-esteem or be insecure. Many have average or above-average self-esteem. Their temperaments are more aggressive and they lack empathy. This can be caused by poor parenting and a lack of good role models or be a personality trait that needs fostering in a positive direction.

A summary of reasons includes:
- They may feel upset or angry or feel they don't fit in.
- They want to seem tough and show off.
- They may get bullied themselves by family members.
- They're scared of getting picked on so do it first.
- If they don't like themselves they may take it out on someone else.
- They think they will become more popular.

The main aim of this scenario is to demonstrate to the students that someone may bully because he/she is jealous of someone else's achievements. Callie actually feels bad about herself and spreads rumors about Jasmine, of whom she is jealous. Students may like to discuss other possible reasons for Callie's actions.

Discussion Points

- How many positive things did Callie write about herself? What else could she have written?
- Why do you think Callie is spreading unkind rumors about Jasmine?
- How do you think Callie really feels?
- How do you think Jasmine feels?
- What could Callie do to make herself feel better?
- Do you think Callie and Jasmine could become friends? Why/Why not?

Did You Know?

Victims of bullying are more likely to tell parents than teachers.

Why Do People Bully? – 4

Jasmine and Callie are in the same class at school. Callie has recently been spreading unkind rumors about Jasmine, although Jasmine has no idea why.

During an English lesson, their teacher asks the class to brainstorm how they feel about themselves. This is what Callie wrote.

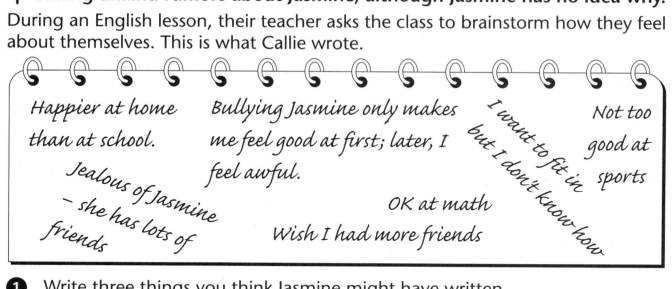

Happier at home than at school.

Bullying Jasmine only makes me feel good at first; later, I feel awful.

I want to fit in but I don't know how

Not too good at sports

Jealous of Jasmine – she has lots of friends

OK at math

Wish I had more friends

1 Write three things you think Jasmine might have written.

2 Use your own words to describe how Callie feels about herself.

_____

3 How could she feel better? _____

_____

4 Suggest a way Callie and Jasmine might become friends.

When I Feel Angry – 1

Teacher's Notes

Indicators

- Identifies situations that make them angry.
- Identifies how being angry makes them feel.

Teacher Information

Showing anger does not necessarily mean someone is displaying bullying behavior. It can become this if behavior is repeated and is physical or verbal to the extreme. Students who bully, however, will more readily adopt aggressive solutions to resolve conflict. They use being angry as an excuse for bullying.

Discussion Points

- Brainstorm situations where students feel anger and list them on the board.
- How does being angry make you feel? What do you look like? What do you do? (Discuss body language.)
- Brainstorm verbs and adjectives to describe anger to assist in Question 2.

Did You Know?

In elementary schools, the students who bully are often in the same grade as the victim. The victim is usually younger, if there is an age difference.

When I Feel Angry – 1

Sometimes people do things that make us feel angry.

❶ Read the sentences below. Check the ones that would make you feel angry. Write one of your own.

- A person you like starts to ignore you. ☐

- Someone won't share with you. ☐

- People don't want to play the same games you do. ☐

- Someone says something about you that you don't like. ☐

- Someone shows off about how many toys he/she owns. ☐

- _____

  _____

❷ Complete the body outline to make it look like you. Write what you look like and how you feel when you are angry.

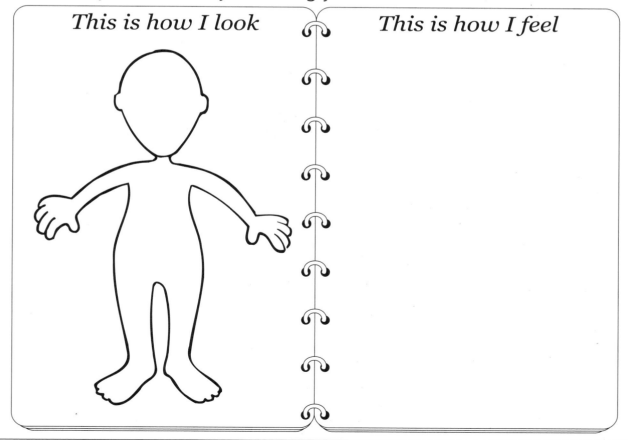

This is how I look   *This is how I feel*

When I Feel Angry – 2

Teacher's Notes

Indicator

- Considers things they can do to control anger.

Teacher Information

Children (or adults) who bully others can come from any kind of family, regardless of social class or cultural background.

People who bully vary in their physical appearance as do the people they bully. A person who bullies is identified by his/her actions.

Encourage students to follow the steps below or their own suggestions on page 35 to help them deal with anger.

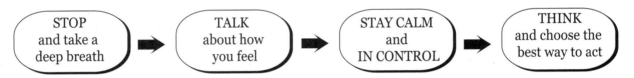

STOP and take a deep breath → TALK about how you feel → STAY CALM and IN CONTROL → THINK and choose the best way to act

Discussion Points

- Is it okay to be angry? Why/Why not?
- What things shouldn't you do when you are angry?
- Have you ever regretted something you have done when you've been angry?
- What are some things you could do to control anger?
- Students could role-play a situation from Question 2 where anger is building up and use steps to control their emotions.

Did You Know?

A child's ability to understand emotions is impaired when he/she witnesses adults showing a lot of anger.

When I Feel Angry – 2

It is okay to feel angry—everyone does sometimes. It's what you do when you feel angry that can be a problem. If you can control what happens when you feel angry, you can avoid doing or saying something that hurts other people.

Here are some things you could practice doing when you feel angry.

- think before you speak
- take deep breaths
- walk away
- say to yourself "I am going to stay calm"
- talk to a friend
- count to 10

1 Suggest some other things you could do when you feel angry.

2 One of the characters in each picture below has started to feel angry with the other character. Write in the speech balloon what you think he/she would be thinking or saying if he/she was trying to control his/her anger.

But I was playing with the ball.

Do you like my new top?

How Does Bullying Make You Feel?

Teacher's Notes

Indicator

- Describes emotions they may feel if they were being bullied.

Teacher Information

Students will differ in their choice of emotions according to how much they are being bullied or are inclined to bully. They should include worry, anger, embarrassment, nervousness, frightened, scared, sad, mad, etc. Being constantly bullied can affect a person's health and/or his/her ability to learn, resulting in short and long-term consequences. These include:

- The stress and feeling of depression may lead to stomach aches or headaches, excessive weeping or crying, bed-wetting, nightmares, or sleeping difficulties.
- Self-esteem drops, along with student's self-image.
- Victims may be reluctant to attend school.

Discussion Points

- Brainstorm positive and negative feelings with students and list situations when they would feel this way. For example, excited – upcoming birthday.

Did You Know?

Physical bullying declines with age, but indirect bullying such as exclusion from groups increases.

How Does Bullying Make You Feel?

Whether it is physical, emotional, or verbal, one of the worst things about being bullied is that it can make you feel bad about yourself.

1 Complete and label the blank faces with emotions you might feel if you were being bullied.

Bullying makes me feel...

2 Write two words to describe how each of these situations might make you feel.

(a) Your best friend suddenly stops wanting to play with you.

(b) You hear some untrue rumors spread about you.

(c) An older student calls you names.

(d) A group of children in your class try to trip you whenever you see them.

3 Write any feeling words on the page you wrote more than once.

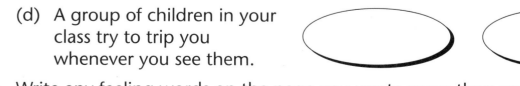

Bullying Feelings

Teacher's Notes

Indicators

- Compares the emotions felt by someone who bullies and someone who is being bullied.
- Compares answers with a classmate.

Teacher Information

Students will differ in their choice of emotions according to how much they are being bullied or are inclined to bully. They should include worry, anger, embarrassment, nervousness, frightened, scared, sad, mad etc. for the victim. The person bullying could be described as angry, powerful, annoyed, bitter, jealous, happy, satisfied, bossy, forceful, strong, etc.

Discussion Points

- What is happening in the picture?
- List keywords and phrases suggested by the students to summarize each situation.
- Which bullying is verbal? Physical? Social?
- What words describe how each person is feeling?
- As a class, discuss the results of Question 3.

Did You Know?

On average, bullying episodes are usually very short, lasting for about 37 seconds.

Bullying Feelings

1 Look at the picture below. Think about how each person might be feeling.

2 Write keywords and phrases to tell how the people involved might feel.

James

Tony

Jessie   Amy

Sarah

Amy

Jessie

Alex

Sam

Shanti

3 Discuss what you wrote with a partner.

- Did you choose similar words or phrases?
- How did the feelings of the people who bullied compare with those being bullied?
- Do you think any of the people in the picture might feel differently about what happened later on?

Bullying Poetry

Teacher's Notes

Indicator

- Expresses emotional and physical reactions to bullying using a poetry framework.

Teacher Information

Students who find it difficult to talk about being bullied may find it easier to express their feelings through creative writing. The exercise should also help students who are not being bullied to understand how it might feel, increasing their empathy for others. Teachers should emphasize that this piece of writing is a private experience and does not have to be shared with others. Students may like to include a picture with their poem, or try other writing forms such as diary or journal entries or letters.

Discussion Points

- How does the poet feel?
- Who do you think the poem is to be read by?
- How did the poem make you feel?
- How do you react to being bullied?
- How could writing your feelings help?
- Before students write their poems, discuss similes, metaphors, alliteration and other poetic devices.
- Discuss other text types students could use to express their feelings.

Did You Know?

Four times out of every five, an argument with someone who bullies will wind up as a physical fight.

Bullying Poetry

1 Read this poem about bullying.

DON'T TRY

Don't try to imagine how I feel
When you push me, lie about me and call me names
Don't try to imagine how I feel
Because I'll tell you
Confusion, sadness, loneliness and anger
Are mixed up inside me
It feels like an icy wind is tearing through my stomach
I want to cry or scream or tell you 'no!'
Don't try to imagine how I feel
Try to imagine how you would feel
If this was happening to you.

2 Use the framework of this poem to write your own poem about bullying.
You can use a situation you have been involved in, or imagine one.
Think about:

(a) Three ways you are being bullied.
(b) Four words to describe what your feelings are.
(c) How your body reacts.
(d) What you feel like doing when you are bullied.

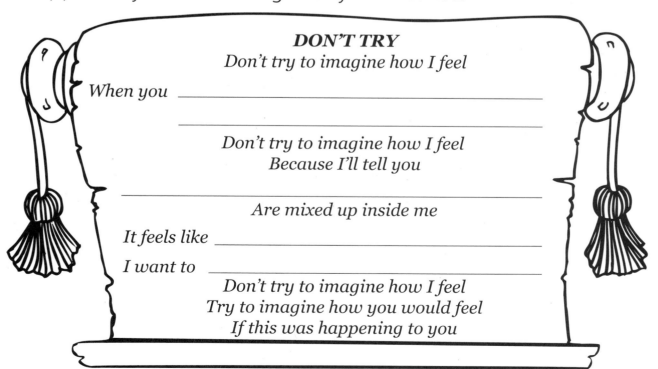

DON'T TRY
Don't try to imagine how I feel
When you _____

_____

Don't try to imagine how I feel
Because I'll tell you

_____
Are mixed up inside me
It feels like _____
I want to _____
Don't try to imagine how I feel
Try to imagine how you would feel
If this was happening to you

Bullying Plays

Teacher's Notes

Indicators

- Understands that the body language of people involved in a bullying situation can influence the outcome.
- Completes simple scripts with appropriate language and actions.

Teacher Information

Students who look unsure of themselves are often targets for bullying. Even using strong words is not effective if the victim's body language shows a lack of confidence. It is important for students to practice looking confident, even if they do not feel that way. Teachers can help by running drama sessions where students participate in exercises where they need to stand confidently, use eye contact and speak clearly. Deep breathing to relax the body can also help.

Discussion Points

- Show a range of pictures of people. Discuss whether they feel good or bad about themselves and why.
- How do you look when you feel good/bad about yourself? Students could draw how they look in both cases.
- Why might people slouch, mumble, etc. when they are feeling bad about themselves? Why might they stand up straight, speak clearly, etc. when they are feeling good about themselves?
- Students could suggest TV or movie characters who look or speak in a certain way. How are they being treated by other characters?
- Introduce the term "body language." Discuss how body language has a bigger impact on people than words.
- Have students try speaking different sentences with different actions, e.g. "Come over here!" with arms folded or arms open. How does the meaning change?

Did You Know?

Body language is an important part of communication. Psychologists say the impact we have on others depends on **what** we say (7%), **how** we say it (38%) and our **body** (nonverbal) language (55%).

Bullying Plays

You are a famous writer who is working on some plays about bullying. One of the things you have to think about is the actions of the characters on stage.

1 Do some research first! Think about what people do when they feel good about themselves and when they feel bad about themselves. Write these reactions under the correct heading below. Add any others.

- *wringing hands*   • *eyes looking down*   • *slouching*   • *mumbling*
- *standing up straight*   • *looking people straight in the eye*
- *chin up*   • *fidgeting*   • *standing solidly*   • *speaking clearly*

Feeling Good

Feeling Bad

2 You are working on two versions of the same play, where the bullied character reacts in two different ways. Write lines for the beginnings of the plays that suit what the character is doing.

 A, wearing new shoes, walks past a group of children who whisper and laugh.

B gets up from the group and stands in front of A.

B   Where did you get your shoes from?

 (A looks terrified and starts to fidget.)

A   _____

B   I think they'd look better dirty. *(B starts to kick sand at A)*

A   *(in a small voice)* _____

 _____

(A moves back and shoulders slouch.)

Bullying Plays

Teacher's Notes

Indicators

- Understands that the body language of people involved in a bullying situation can influence the outcome.
- Completes simple scripts with appropriate language and actions.

Teacher Information

Students who look unsure of themselves are often targets for bullying. Even using strong words is not effective if the victim's body language shows a lack of confidence. It is important for students to practice looking confident, even if they do not feel that way. Teachers can help by running drama sessions where students participate in exercises where they need to stand confidently, use eye contact and speak clearly. Deep breathing to relax the body can also help.

Discussion Points

- Show a range of pictures of people. Discuss whether they feel good or bad about themselves and why.
- How do you look when you feel good/bad about yourself? Students could draw how they look in both cases.
- Why might people slouch, mumble, etc. when they are feeling bad about themselves? Why might they stand up straight, speak clearly, etc. when they are feeling good about themselves?
- Students could suggest TV or movie characters who look or speak in a certain way. How are they being treated by other characters?
- Introduce the term "body-language." Discuss how body language has a bigger impact on people than words.
- Have students try speaking different sentences with different actions e.g. "Come over here!" with arms folded or arms open. How does the meaning change?

Did You Know?

Boys are more likely to use physical forms of bullying; girls are more likely to use put-downs, spread rumors, practice social exclusion, or use rejection or ostracism.

Bullying Plays

A, wearing new shoes, walks past a group of children who whisper and laugh.
B gets up from the group and stands in front of A.

B   Where did you get your shoes from?

(A looks B solidly in the eye and stands solidly on the ground.)

A   _____

B   I think they'd look better dirty. *(B starts to kick sand at A)*

A   *(in a firm voice)* _____

_____

(A stands up straight, turns around and walks away.)

3   Do you think the plays will end differently? Why/Why not?

_____

_____

4   Try adding character actions for the beginning of this play. You could use actions that show the character is feeling only bad or good about himself/herself, or use a mixture!

A   *Hi, B. I've got an invitation here for my party.*

B   *Sorry, I can't come.* (A _____

_____)

A   *But you don't know when it is yet.* (A _____

_____)

B   *I don't want to come to your stupid party. Give me the invitation and I'll put it in the waste basket.*

5   How do you think this play will end?

_____

_____

6   Try acting the beginnings of the plays with a small group. Make up some suitable endings.

⟨ **What Should You Do?** ⟩

Teacher's Notes 🧍🧍🧍

Indicator

- Considers courses of action that could be taken if someone is bullied.

Teacher Information

It is imperative students realize that bullying is not to be tolerated and they should not put up with it if it is happening to them.

The worksheet gives students some steps to tackle bullying.

These are some things the students should **not** do.
1. Try to keep dealing with the problem themselves – it is all right to ask for help.
2. Exaggerate or not tell the true facts. If a part of what they say is shown to be untrue, it casts doubt upon the whole situation.
3. Retaliate by hitting, etc. They could end up being accused of bullying.

Discussion Points

- Discuss how everyone has the right to feel safe and that no one deserves to be bullied.
- What should you do if you are bullied? What might happen if you don't do something about it?
- Discuss being a "tattletale." Why is it seen as "uncool" to tell a teacher about bullying? Why is it important to tell? Discuss how people who bully rely on secrecy.
- What is wrong with some things people do to deal with being bullied? Discuss safety.

Did You Know?

Most victims will not tell anyone they are being bullied.

What Should You Do?

Find a group of three or four people to discuss the ideas on this page. Many people feel helpless when they are being bullied, but there are some things you can do in any situation.

- **Stay calm and look confident** – *even if you don't feel this way, you can pretend.*
- **Speak loudly and firmly** *to the person/people bullying you – say that you don't like what is happening and tell them to stop.*
- **Don't be mean back** – *it will not make bullying go away.*
- **Get away** *from the situation – find some friends or go to a safe place.*
- **Tell an adult** *about it.*

1 Which of these steps would be the most difficult to do? Why?

_____

2 Write words to describe how your group feels about telling an adult.

_____

3 Imagine you are given these additional pieces of advice by a friend. Write the group's opinion on these in the table and then report to the class.

Advice	Opinion
Use humor – make the person bullying you laugh!	
Agree with everything the person bullying you says.	
Make friends with the person bullying you.	
Yell and scream as loudly as you can.	
Trick the person bullying you; e.g., say that you have a black belt in karate.	

School Report

Teacher's Notes

Indicator

- Evaluates own behavior when dealing with being bullied, using a report format.

Teacher Information

Students should examine their behavior in the context of information learned from the "What Should You Do?" worksheet.

Discussion Points

- Review the three types of bullying – verbal, physical, social and their meanings.
- Encourage the students to be as positive as possible about their behavior when completing the report.
- How well do you cope/think you would cope with being bullied?
- Which type of bullying would you find most difficult to cope with?

Did You Know?

When people who bully in elementary school grow up, they will need more government support, have more court convictions, be more likely to be alcoholics, will be more antisocial and need more mental health care.

School Report

Welcome to the School of Friendship. All teachers have to report on how their students would deal with being bullied.

Imagine you are one of these teachers. Write a report about yourself.

Name: _____ Year: _____

General Behavior

Check the correct box for each statement about the student's behavior.

	Sometimes	Always	Never
• Walks confidently	☐	☐	☐
• Tells adults if bullied	☐	☐	☐
• Tells the person bullying to stop	☐	☐	☐
• Controls his/her anger	☐	☐	☐
• Leaves a bullying situation quickly	☐	☐	☐

Types of Bullying

Write about and color the correct face to describe how the student would react to different types of bullying.

Overall Comments

Type of Bullying	Comment	Assessment
Verbal (e.g. name calling, teasing)		☺ ☺ ☹
Physical (e.g., kicking, pushing)		☺ ☺ ☹
Social (e.g., being ignored, being left out of a group)		☺ ☺ ☹

When in a bullying situation, _____

is best at _____

He/She could improve at _____

Dear Problem Solver

Teacher's Notes

Indicator

- Suggests ways of dealing with bullying scenarios in a letter format.

Teacher Information

It is imperative students realize that bullying is not to be tolerated and they should not put up with it if it is happening to them.

The worksheet gives students some suggestions to tackle bullying.

These are some things the students should **not** do.
1. Try to keep dealing with the problem themselves – it is all right to ask for help.
2. Exaggerate or not tell the true facts. If a part of what they say is shown to be untrue, it casts doubt upon the whole situation.
3. Retaliate by hitting, etc. They could end up being accused of bullying.
   Students should have a copy of the "What Should You Do?" worksheet to help them with this activity.

Discussion Points

- What types of bullying are described in the letters?
- Discuss issues that are brought up in the letters, such as prejudice, peer pressure, fear and lack of confidence.
- Have you or a friend ever had a problem similar to any outlined in the letters? What happened?
- Which writer has the most serious problem? Why?
- Discuss each writer's behavior and how each could change what he/she is doing to improve the situation.
- After the sheet is completed, discuss all answers. Remind students that there is no perfect solution to bullying.

Did You Know?

Many adults do not know how to intervene in bullying situations; therefore, bullying is overlooked.

Dear Problem Solver

Read these letters from the problem pages of a magazine.

Dear Problem Solver

I am friends with a group of girls who don't like another girl in our class. I think it's because she's very smart and good at her schoolwork. I usually go along with what the group does to her because I want to stay friends with them. We usually call her names and ignore her. She is having a birthday party soon and has invited everyone in the class. The leader of our group has told everyone not to go. I actually quite like this girl and I am sick of being mean to her. What should I do? I don't want the group to start bullying me.

Grace

Dear Problem Solver

I sit next to a boy who kicks me whenever the teacher is not looking. I can't ask the teacher to move me, because I am the smallest person in the class and everyone thinks I am weak already. I have told this boy that it hurts me, but it only comes out as a whisper. I don't know who I can tell. What should I do?

Jack

Dear Problem Solver

I am usually very happy at school, but lately I feel miserable. Because of my religion I wear a turban. Other kids in my class are used to it, but a new kid has arrived who teases me about it. He has made a group of friends and he always makes sure they are around before he says anything. He also passes notes about me in class. I've tried shouting at him. I haven't told anyone about it.

Satish

❶ Discuss each problem with a partner.

❷ Write a reply to each letter on a separate sheet of paper.

    Hints: • Suggest why what the writer is doing is not working.

           • Suggest some things he/she could do.

           • Remember: There is no perfect solution to bullying!

Who Can Help Me?

Teacher's Notes

Indicator

- Comprehends why telling an adult about bullying is important.
- Plans each aspect of what to tell an adult about a bullying situation.

Teacher Information

Students may be reluctant to inform a teacher about bullying because they:
- do not want to be labeled as "tattletales"
- think it will make it worse
- feel that teachers can't or won't be able to help them

Students must realize bullying is not to be tolerated and that the only way to stop bullying is to be open about it with actions or words. Keeping it a secret from adults they trust gives the bullies more power to continue. That is why they go to so much trouble to try to stop victims from telling.

Students should also realize the importance of telling the truth. If a part of what they say is untrue it casts doubt on the situation. They must also differentiate between a friendly tease as opposed to an intentionally upsetting remark that continues.

Discussion Points

- Why is it important to tell an adult about bullying? Why might it be difficult to do this? What could help make it easier?
- How could telling an adult help someone who is being bullied?
- What should you do if the adult can't or won't help?
- Discuss the statement "People who bully rely on keeping their behavior a secret."
- Which adults would you tell if you were bullied? Why?
- Practice role-playing telling an adult about bullying. Discuss how successful each role play was at getting across a clear message. What were the features of the most successful role plays?

Did You Know?

Over 70% of teachers say they always intervene in a bullying situation but only 25% of students agree with them!

Who Can Help Me?

Students often don't want to tell an adult if they are being bullied. They might feel it is being a "tattletale," that the bully will find out or that no one can help. But it is important to tell if bullying is making you feel miserable and unsafe.

Often, schools can put a stop to bullying without the bully finding out who has told. Even if the person who bullies does find out, it is better to have it out in the open. People who bully rely on keeping their behavior a secret.

Adults can do many things to help stop bullying. They can talk to the person who is bullying you or give you advice. Choose an adult you trust, and if you feel scared, ask a friend to come with you. If that adult doesn't help, then keep speaking up until someone does.

If you are a person who bullies and you want to stop, it can also help to talk to an adult. They can talk to you about why you bully and suggest how you can stop.

1 Complete these sentences.

(a) It is important to tell an adult if I am being bullied because

_____.

(b) If the person who bullies finds out I have told _____

_____.

(c) Three adults I could tell if I was being bullied are

_____.

2 When you tell an adult about bullying, you need to tell him or her *who* is bullying/being bullied, *what* happens, *how often* it happens, *where* it happens and your *feelings*. Think of a bullying situation and write the answers in the boxes. You can answer as either a person who is bullying or who is being bullied.

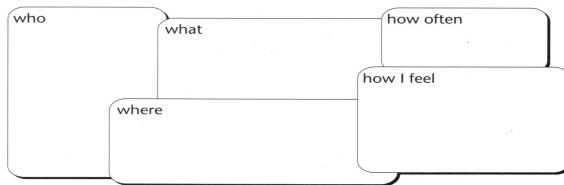

who

what

how often

how I feel

where

How Can I Help?

Teacher's Notes

Indicator

- Considers appropriate ways to help someone who is being bullied.

Teacher Information

Students who witness bullying may act in the following ways:
- Help the person bullying by joining in.
- Help the person bullying by watching, laughing, or shouting encouragement.
- Remain completely uninvolved.
- Help the person being bullied by telling the person bullying to stop or getting an adult, etc.

Bullying usually happens where the person doing the bullying has an "audience" of other children. It might be people he/she doesn't know or a group of friends. If adults are nearby, though, bullies can be very careful at not letting them see what they are doing.

When a group of people bully, there is often a "leader" and "followers" who go along with what the leader is doing or saying. Sometimes the followers do not really agree with what the leader is doing, but might feel that they have to. This is sometimes called "peer pressure."

Openly discussing ways for students to assist others who are being bullied will help foster an anti-bullying attitude in the school.

Discussion Points

- Why is it important to help someone who is being bullied?
- What could you do to help someone who is being bullied?
- Discuss the importance of staying safe when attempting to help someone.
- Are there some things you shouldn't do to help someone? Why?
- Why might a person avoid helping someone who is being bullied?
- In what kind of situation would you find it the most difficult to help someone else? Why?
- If the issue has not already been raised, discuss the influence peer pressure has on determining whether someone helps or not.

Did You Know?

Playground statistics have shown that – every seven minutes a child is bullied – adult intervention – 4%, peer intervention 11% – no intervention 85%.

How Can I Help?

1 Read this information leaflet on bullying.

Have you ever seen someone being bullied? Did you try to help or did you think that there was nothing you could do? The problem with doing nothing is that we let people who bully get away with their behavior. There are some things you can do to help someone being bullied while staying safe yourself.

These include:
- Refusing to join in with the bullying.
- Getting an adult.
- Telling the bully to stop with the support of other people.
- Trying to be a friend to the person being bullied.

You should never try to take on the bully—it is not safe and could lead you into bullying behavior, too!

2 Would this advice change your behavior? Explain.

3 Draw yourself next to the speech and thought balloons. Write what you would be saying and thinking. Consider how you are helping and how you are staying safe.

4 Discuss reasons for what you drew and wrote.

What Makes a Good Friend?

Teacher's Notes

Indicator

- Understands the importance of being friendly to others.

Teacher Information

When a student is new to a school it can be hard to make friends and find a group to fit in with. Some students may play on a new student's insecurity and pick on or even bully him/her. Encouraging and discussing ways students could interact with new students helps create a positive, welcoming atmosphere, with students being more open and understanding of how newcomers may be feeling. Thinking of and doing "acts of kindness" helps promote a positive, caring atmosphere in the school. Negative acts such as bullying will be less tolerated as "acts of kindness" become second nature.

Discussion Points

- What makes a good friend?
- What does it mean to be friendly?
- "If I don't like someone I don't have to be friendly to them!" Discuss.
- Discuss how being friendly can have a positive effect on both the giver and the receiver.
- If everyone was friendly to each other, would bullying exist? Give reasons for your answer.
- Discuss the concept of "acts of kindness."
- How could you make a new person at your school feel welcome?

Did You Know?

Children of bullies often become bullies themselves and will probably continue to bully as adults unless they get help.

What Makes a Good Friend?

1 Brainstorm words and phrases to describe ways of *not* being friendly.

2 Now write words and phrases to describe ways of being friendly.

listens shares kind smiles FRIEND

3 Discuss the questions below before writing an answer.

(a) Do you have to be friends with everyone?

Why/Why not ? _____

(b) Should you be friendly towards everyone?

Why/Why not ? _____

(c) How do you feel if someone acts in an unfriendly way to you?

_____

_____

When you care about other people they will care about you. It is easy to do and say nice things to another, even if he/she is not a special friend.

4 Write things you could do and say to someone in your class who is not a special friend?

Do ...

Say ...

Mediation

Teacher's Notes

Indicators

- Understands the concept of peer mediation and its benefits.
- Role-plays peer mediation situations.

Teacher Information

Peer mediation uses discussion to resolve minor conflicts between two students with the help of a professionally trained student mediator. It is based on the belief that resolutions are best reached with the help of a neutral third party and that students are more honest with and more likely to listen to peers than adults when discussing conflict. Common conflicts peer mediators face include name-calling, rumors, taking property without asking, teasing and invading personal space.

Peer mediators are trained to attack the problem, rather than the people involved. They encourage the parties to treat each other with respect. During the discussion, each person is required to state the problem, describe his/her feelings and say how he/she is responsible for the problem. Possible solutions are then brainstormed, and a fair solution that suits both parties is reached.

A successful peer mediation program can enhance communication and problem-solving skills, create a more comfortable school environment and encourage tolerance of others. It can also be empowering for students because they are assuming a greater responsibility for their own problems.
Peer mediation should only be attempted in a school where staff and students have attended a training course. Details of courses in peer mediation can be found on the Internet. Try typing "school mediation courses" into a search engine.

Discussion Points

- Discuss how students usually solve problems they have with others.
- How could a third person help to solve a problem between two people? What qualities would he/she need to have?
- What is a "peer"?
- Discuss the reasons for, and the benefits of, peer mediation.
- What does "compromise" mean? Discuss how compromising may need to happen to resolve a conflict.

Did You Know?

8% of students miss one day of school a month to avoid being bullied.

Mediation

If you have a disagreement or problem with someone else, you might need a third person to help you sort it out. This person is called a mediator. Mediators are trained to help two people solve a problem. They do not judge anyone's behavior. A good mediator listens to both sides of the story. Mediators help people to communicate by following these steps.

- **Agree:** *Ask the two people to agree that they want to solve the problem.*
- **Set the rules:** *The two people should agree to listen to each other's opinions. They should not interrupt, yell or put each other down. They should always tell the truth.*
- **The problem:** *Ask both people to explain what the problem is and how it makes them feel. Encourage each person to say how he/she is responsible for the problem.*
- **Brainstorm:** *All three people brainstorm solutions to the problem.*
- **Discuss solutions:** *Everyone discusses each solution. The mediator helps the two people decide if one is fair and sensible.*
- **Decide on a solution:** *Everyone decides on a fair solution that makes both people happy. This might involve each person compromising or giving way a bit.*

- Find a group of three people to act in three short mediation role plays. Each person in your group should act as the mediator in one play. The mediator should follow the steps above to help solve each problem.

- Plan each drama first by deciding on:
  - the characters
  - how the situation started
  - how the play will end

PROBLEM 1: One person is taking the other's lunch money every day.

PROBLEM 2: One person is spreading rumors about the other.

PROBLEM 3: Make up your own!

Learning to be Confident

Teacher's Notes

Indicators

- Identifies confident behavior.
- Brainstorms positive thoughts about themselves and confident actions.

Teacher Information

Students who look unsure of themselves are often targets for bullying. Even using strong words is not effective if the victims' body language shows a lack of confidence. It is important for students to practice looking confident, even if they do not feel that way. Teachers can help by running drama sessions where students participate in exercises where they need to stand confidently, use eye contact and speak clearly. Deep breathing to relax the body can also help.

Discussion Points

- What makes you feel good about yourself? What makes you feel bad about yourself? Discuss which things are in the students' control to change for the better.
- What does "confidence" mean?
- Do you think it is possible to feel confident? Why/Why not?
- What special qualities do you have?
- Discuss what changes in students' lives when they feel confident.

Did You Know?

There are three ways of responding to bullying: being passive, aggressive, or assertive. Generally, people who bully tend to be aggressive while their victims tend to be passive.

Learning to be Confident

People who bully are more likely to pick on someone they think is timid or quiet and who doesn't look confident.

1 Look at these two students below. Write keywords and phrases about how each looks and what he/she might be feeling.

 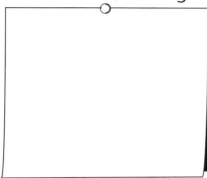  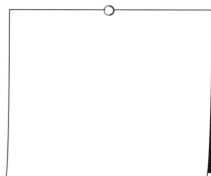

Confident people feel good about themselves—about the way they look and about the type of people they are.

2 To practice feeling confident, you could try some of these things.

Write a list of things you do best. When someone says something nice about you, add that to your list. Read over the list from time to time, especially when you are feeling down.

Start your list here.

_____

_____

_____

Practice talking about yourself in a positive way. For example, instead of saying "I hate my freckles," you could say "Lots of people have freckles, even movie stars!"

Write an example you could say about yourself.

_____

_____

Practice being clear and sure about what you want to say to people, especially when they are doing something you don't like. For example, if someone keeps using your markers without asking, instead of thinking "I wish he wouldn't do that," you could say "I'd like you to ask if you can use my markers."

Write an example here.

_____

_____

_____

_____

Tolerance

Teacher's Notes

Indicators

- Develops an understanding of tolerance and human rights in a classroom context.
- Designs and creates a "classroom rights" poster.

Teacher Information

Teaching children tolerance is also teaching them not to hate. Teachers can teach tolerance most effectively by modeling tolerant behavior in the classroom and playground.

Discussion Points

- What does "tolerance" mean?
- Why is it important to be tolerant of others? Does it mean you have to agree with everyone's beliefs?
- Discuss the outcomes of tolerant behavior in children and adults.
- What rights should everyone have?

Did You Know?

Children seem to give positive attention to the bully rather than the victim.

Tolerance

Tolerance means respecting others, no matter what they look like or what they believe. This doesn't mean you have to agree with them, but that you accept that everyone is different. Remember—the world would be a boring place if everyone was the same!

A good place to start practicing tolerance is in your classroom. How can everyone be treated fairly and safely? Use this page to plan a poster that sets out the rights everyone in the classroom should have.

1 Brainstorm how the people in your class could treat each other better.

2 Find a partner. Use both lists of ideas to write two rights you feel are the most important; for example, "the right to learn without interruption."

The Right to ...

The Right to ...

3 Share your ideas with the class. Choose the four most common rights. Write them below.

Our Rights

The right to _____

The right to _____

The right to _____

The right to _____

4 Write what you will draw on your poster.

_____

5 Create your poster on a large sheet of paper.

Cooperation and Communication Games

Teacher's Notes

Indicator

- Participates in class and small-group drama games which require communication and cooperation.

Teacher Information

Drama games are a positive and fun way to promote cooperation and communication in the classroom. The six games on the next page are easy to set up, and can be used to begin a drama session or as a class reward. For the games involving small-group interaction, encourage students to work with those who may not be their friends.

Discussion Points

- Sculptures – Emphasize the importance of clear and precise instructions. Foster an attitude of fun, rather than frustration.
- Applause – Encourage patience and working together. A discussion after the game about the importance of verbal communication may be valuable; e.g.. "How much quicker would this game have been if we had been able to speak?"
- Class Scene – Emphasize the importance of the cooperation among the small groups on the "set" to make the scene work. This game is challenging!
- Number Swap – Emphasize the fact that each member of the group must stay silent or the game will not work.
- Physical Relay – Depending on the class, you may like to emphasize the importance of completing the relay correctly rather than the speed.

Did You Know?

Unless new behaviors are adopted, students who bully will continue to do so. By 24, up to 60% of children who bully will have at least one criminal conviction.

Cooperation and Communication Games

Sculptures

Students make groups of three. The teacher decides on a shape for a student "sculpture" (e.g., right arm in the air, standing on left leg, etc.). The teacher tells two people in each group this instruction. They then tell the third and fourth people in their groups. The third person has to help the fourth person into the shape without looking at other groups.

Shapes

Students move around the room. On a signal, they form groups of three or four and make the shape of an object – such as a rowing boat, a computer, etc. Do this four or five times, with students working with different people each time. Finally, call out the names of the objects. Students have to remember exactly where they were and who they worked with and form the shapes again.

Applause

One student leaves the room. The rest of the class choose an object the person has to walk to and whether he/she should jump, sit, stretch up or kneel when there. When the student comes back, he/she has to find out what the class wants him/her to do. The class can only communicate through applause—the closer the student gets, the more claps. When he/she gets it right, there should be thunderous applause and a standing ovation!

Physical Relay

Students form small, equal groups. Each group sits in a line and follows instructions for a relay. Each student in the line has different task. For example:

Student 1, pat 2 on the head

Student 2, spin around and tag 3, etc.

When the line has finished, the last person comes to the front. Repeat until the students are back to their start positions.

Class Scene

Ask the class to make a "frozen" scene from an action movie; e.g., a pirate ship, a robbery, etc. Two students can be the directors, and they put the others into various positions around the "set." Encourage lots of different characters. The whole scene can then come to life with students repeating simple lines and actions as the teacher uses a "remote control" to fast forward, pause, rewind, etc. Students have to cooperate to make the scene work.

Number Swap

The class sits in a circle. Give each student a number, counting from 1. The students then swap places in the circle so they are mixed up. Choose two students to blindfold and have them stand in the middle of circle. Each calls out a number. The students with these numbers have to swap places in the circle without getting tagged by the blindfolded students. The other students have to agree to stay silent and to watch out for the blindfolded students.

Notes

Notes

Notes

Notes

Notes

Notes

Notes